X-TREME FACTS:

T0011487

PLANETS AND MOONS

by Catherine C. Finan

BEARPORT
PUBLISHING

Minneapolis, Minnesota

Credits:

Cover, NASA images/Shutterstock, Panparinda/Shutterstock, Nutkamol komolvanich/Shutterstock, alexaldo/Shutterstock, NASA, alexaldo/Shutterstock, Martin Holverda/iStock, Klever_ok/Shutterstock; Title Page, DanieleGay/Shutterstock; 4–5, Computer Earth/Shutterstock; 4 bottom right, ViDI Studio/Shutterstock; 5 top, Johan Swanepoel/Shutterstock; 5 bottom right, Creativa Images/Shutterstock; 6 top, Vadim Sadovski/Shutterstock; 6 bottom, 21 top, Dotted Yeti/Shutterstock; 7 top, NASA/JPL-Caltech/Public Domain; 7 bottom, 14, NASA images/Shutterstock; 8 top, 9 top, 11 top right, 12 top left, 13 bottom right, 15, 16, 17 top, 17 middle, 18 top, 19 middle, 22 top, 23 top, 23 middle, 24 top, 25 top, 25 bottom right, 26, 27, 27 top, 28 top left, NASA/Public Domain; 8 bottom, 9 bottom, Johan Swanepoel/Shutterstock; 9 middle, NASA, JPL Multimission Image Processing Laboratory, U.S Geological Survey/Public Domain; 9 bottom right, Gelpi/Shutterstock; 10, Guitar photographer/Shutterstock; 10 middle, Triff/Shutterstock; 10 bottom, Design Projects/Shutterstock; 11 top, Michelangelus/Shutterstock; 11 middle, Johan Swanepoel/Shutterstock; 11 bottom, Eric Isselee/Shutterstock; 11 bottom right, Twinsterphoto/Shutterstock; 12 bottom, gianni triggiani/Shutterstock; 12 bottom right, 17 bottom right, 28–29, Austen Photography; 13 top, 13 bottom left, NASA/Neil A. Armstrong/Public Domain; 13 bottom, Mopic/Shutterstock; 14 bottom left, Jean-Pol GRANDMONT/Creative Commons; 15 bottom left, 15 bottom right, 18 bottom left, Merlin74/Shutterstock; 17 bottom, WitR/Shutterstock; 17 bottom left, izikMD/Shutterstock; 18–19 Jurik Peter/Shutterstock; 18 bottom right, I, Sailko/Creative Commons; 19 top, 3d_vicka/Shutterstock; 19 middle, freestyle images/Shutterstock; 19 bottom right, stocksolutions/Shutterstock; 20 top, Oliver Denker/Shutterstock; 20 bottom right, Yuri Turkov/Shutterstock.com; 21 middle, sdecoret/Shutterstock; 21 bottom, HQuality/Shutterstock; 22 bottom left, LightField Studios/Shutterstock; 22 bottom right, Aviad Bublil/Creative Commons; 23 middle left, Justin Cowart/Creative Commons; 23 bottom, Keitma/Shutterstock; 23 bottom middle, Oqbas/Shutterstock; 23 bottom off right, Kuznetsov Alexey/Shutterstock; 23 bottom right, Erik Lam/Shutterstock; 24 bottom right, Cristiano Banti/Public Domain; 25 top left, Ismoon/Creative Commons; 25 middle left, NASA/JPL/SSI/Gordan Ugarkovic/Public Domain; 25 middle right, NASA/JPL-Caltech; 25 bottom left, Joe Seer/Shutterstock.com; 26 bottom left, Paul Michael Hughes/Shutterstock; 26 bottom right, Anna Om/Shutterstock; 27 middle, NASA/Goddard/Francis Reddy/Public Domain; 27 bottom, Design Projects/Shutterstock; 28 bottom left, Bardocz Peter/Shutterstock; 28 bottom middle, Be Good/Shutterstock;

President: Jen Jenson
Director of Product Development: Spencer Brinker
Senior Editor: Allison Juda
Associate Editor: Charly Haley
Designer: Elena Klinkner

Developed and produced for Bearport Publishing by BlueAppleWorks Inc.
Managing Editor for BlueAppleWorks: Melissa McClellan
Art Director: T.J. Choleva
Photo Research: Jane Reid

Library of Congress Cataloging-in-Publication Data

Names: Finan, Catherine C., 1972- author.
Title: Planets and moons / by Catherine C. Finan.
Description: Minneapolis, Minnesota : Bearport Publishing, [2022] | Series:
    X-treme facts: space | Includes bibliographical references and index.
Identifiers: LCCN 2021026702 (print) | LCCN 2021026703 (ebook) | ISBN
    9781636915098 (library binding) | ISBN 9781636915166 (paperback) | ISBN
    9781636915234 (ebook)
Subjects: LCSH: Planets--Juvenile literature. | Satellites--Juvenile
    literature.
Classification: LCC QB602 .F563 2022 (print) | LCC QB602 (ebook) | DDC
    523.4--dc23
LC record available at https://lccn.loc.gov/2021026702
LC ebook record available at https://lccn.loc.gov/2021026703

For more information, write to Bearport Publishing, 5357 Penn Avenue South, Minneapolis, MN 55419.
Printed in the United States of America.

Contents

Planets and Moons

The night sky is scattered with shining stars. But there are some surprises mixed in with the glowing dots. If you were to get closer to the things that shine extra bright, you may see that they aren't stars—they're planets! There are eight planets in our solar system. And among these planets are more than 200 moons. Let's go on a solar system adventure to learn more!

Mercury **orbits** closest to the sun, followed by Venus, Earth, Mars, Jupiter, Saturn, Uranus, and Neptune.

I'M SMALL BUT MIGHTY!

Sun

Mercury

Venus

Earth

Mars

MIGHTY OR NOT, EARTH IS THE COOLEST!

All eight planets in our solar system orbit around the sun. The sun's **gravity** keeps the planets on their paths.

Earth has one moon. It is about 238,800 miles (384,300 km) away from us.

I GUESS YOU'RE STUCK WITH ME, MOON. MY GRAVITY IS KEEPING YOU CLOSE!

WELL, THAT'S TRUE, BUT I CAN STILL RUN CIRCLES AROUND YOU!

Gravity also keeps moons orbiting around their planets.

I'M KING OF THE PLANETS!

Saturn

Uranus

Neptune

Jupiter

IF YOU WANT TO TRAVEL IN SPACE, YOU'LL HAVE TO *PLANET*!

Jupiter is the largest planet. It's so big that more than 1,300 Earths would fit inside it.

Our solar system, including the sun, planets, and moons, formed about 4.5 billion years ago. Now that's old!

5

Rockin' Planets

Billions of years ago, our solar system was just a cloud of gas and dust. Then, the cloud became a swirling **disk** of **material**. Gravity pulled material to the center of the disk and formed a very hot star—the sun. Gravity also pulled together material to form the planets. Some planets are made of rock, and others are made mostly of gas. The rocky planets formed closer to the sun because they could handle the sun's heat. That's why Mercury, Venus, Earth, and Mars are really rockin'!

The rocky planets are small compared to the much larger, colder gas planets that are way out past Mars.

LET'S ROCK!

Mercury

Venus

Earth

Mars

Earth is the only planet we know of where living things can survive.

Mercury is the smallest planet. It's just a little bit bigger than Earth's moon.

I'M ROCKING WITH THE BIG GUYS!

Mars is sometimes called the Red Planet. It gets its color from rusty iron in its soil.

Even though it is closest to the sun, Mercury is not the hottest planet. Venus wins that honor. Its thick **atmosphere** traps the sun's heat.

The Sun's Nearest Neighbors

Although Mercury is closest to the sun, this crater-covered planet is still about 36 million miles (58 million km) away. From there, it's more than 31 million miles (50 million km) to reach the next planet, Venus, which is covered in mountains and volcanoes. What else do we know about the sun's two closest neighbors?

Even though Mercury is close to the hot sun, **some of its craters may have ice in them.**

Mercury's craters formed when **asteroids** and other space objects hit the planet.

Venus's hot atmosphere is full of **carbon dioxide** and yellowish clouds of **acid** that would be deadly to humans. *Yikes!*

I THOUGHT BEING A VENUS VOLCANO MADE ME SPECIAL! BUT I'M JUST ONE OF THE MANY . . .

Venus has the most volcanoes of any planet in our solar system.

The gases around Venus are so **thick** that walking there would feel like walking through water.

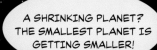

Mercury and Venus are the only planets in our solar system without any moons.

A SHRINKING PLANET? THE SMALLEST PLANET IS GETTING SMALLER!

Mercury is slowly shrinking. Scientists have found that over the past 4 billion years, the planet got at least one mile (1.6 km) smaller across.

What's So Great about Earth?

From Venus, it's another 25.7 million miles (41.4 million km) to our home planet, Earth! Earth orbits the sun in a special area called the Goldilocks zone, which is not too hot and not too cold. The planet's temperature, atmosphere, and water make it the only place in our solar system that's just right for life as we know it. And that's just some of what makes our planet awesome!

About 70 percent of Earth is covered by water.

THIS PLANET LOOKS A BIT CHUBBY AROUND THE MIDDLE.

MAYBE IT'S BECAUSE OF ALL THAT WATER!

Earth is not a perfect **sphere**. It's flatter at the top and bottom and bulges out more in the middle.

It takes more than eight minutes for light from the sun to reach Earth.

I'M SORRY TO KEEP YOU WAITING, EARTH!

NO PROBLEM. I CAN HANDLE AN EIGHT-MINUTE WAIT!

Earth is the only planet in our solar system with just one moon.

Earth's **core** is as hot as the surface of the sun.

Scientists think there could be as many as a **trillion different kinds of living things** on Earth.

I'M ONE IN A TRILLION.

BIG DEAL, SO AM I!

MMM, OXYGEN. THANKS, EARTH!

Earth is the only planet with an atmosphere humans can breathe. People need **oxygen**, and our atmosphere's got it!

To the Moon!

Earth's moon is a familiar sight for many of us when we look at the night sky. But how did it get there? Not long after our solar system formed, Earth probably smashed into another planet-sized object. Pieces of Earth and the other object were thrown into space. Gravity pulled them together to form our beautiful moon.

We see the moon glowing in the sky. But the moon doesn't make its own light—it reflects light from the sun.

The moon is about **one-quarter the size of Earth.**

DON'T I LOOK GOOD IN THIS LIGHT?

AWESOME! LET ME TAKE A PICTURE FOR OUR SCIENCE PROJECT!

Of all the planets and moons, Earth's moon is the only one that humans have ever traveled to.

Twelve astronauts have walked on the moon.

TALK ABOUT FAR OUT, NEIL!

On July 20, 1969, American astronauts Neil Armstrong and Buzz Aldrin became the first people to step on the moon.

Scientists have found frozen water deep inside some of the craters on the moon.

WHERE ARE YOU GOING?

I'M THIRSTY. I'M GOING TO DIG UP SOME ICE WATER!

Mighty Mars

Next up is Mars! Because the Red Planet is about 142 million miles (228.5 million km) from the sun, it gets pretty chilly. Mars is a cold desert planet, but—like Earth—it has canyons, volcanoes, and polar ice caps. There's a thin atmosphere with clouds, and strong winds can whip up the red, dusty soil. Sometimes, dust storms cover the whole planet. Better take cover!

Mars is named for the Roman god of war because its red color looks like the blood from battles.

On a clear night, Mars' reddish glow can be seen from Earth without a telescope.

RED'S A GREAT COLOR ON YOU, MARS!

THANKS, MARS!

Mars has the tallest volcano in our solar system. It's three times the height of Mount Everest.

Mars has two moons, Phobos and Deimos. Their names are Greek. *Phobos* means *fear*, and *Deimos* means *panic*.

We've sent vehicles called **rovers** to explore Mars. **Scientists hope to send people to the Red Planet one day!**

Scientists have found signs of flowing water on Mars. This might mean Mars could support living things.

Feeling Gassy?

Beyond the rocky Red Planet are the gas planets—Jupiter, Saturn, Uranus, and Neptune. These planets formed in the cold of our outer solar system, where the sun's heat couldn't burn away their gases. They grew and became even larger than our rocky planets. And because they're made mostly of gas, these planets have no solid ground to stand on! Let's take a closer look at these mysterious, gassy places.

JUPITER, JUMP OVER THE BELT AND COME FOR A CHAT!

An asteroid belt fills the space between rocky Mars and gassy Jupiter. It has millions of asteroids!

I'D BETTER NOT, MARS. I'M FEELING GASSY!

Jupiter's surface has fierce weather. There are hurricane-like storms with strong winds, thunder, and lightning.

Saturn has beautiful rings made of ice chunks and rocks that orbit the planet.

GASSY OR NOT, I'M BEAUTIFUL!

In 1781, Uranus became the first planet discovered with a telescope. Before then, **astronomers** had to spot planets with their eyes alone.

Neptune is named for the Roman god of the sea. A gas called methane makes it look blue like water.

I'VE FOUND URANUS UP THERE, IN THE SKY!

WHAT ARE YOU TALKING ABOUT? IT'S RIGHT HERE!

Gee, They're Giant!

Jupiter, our solar system's fifth planet, is a whopping 484 million miles (778 million km) from the sun. It's not just the largest planet—it's also 2.5 times heavier than all the other planets in our solar system combined! Another 402 million miles (647 million km) beyond Jupiter is the second-largest planet, Saturn. Its dazzling rings are an incredible sight.

Jupiter has a huge storm that's lasted for hundreds of years!

It rains diamonds on both Jupiter and Saturn.

WOULD YOU MIND IF I GATHERED SOME RAIN FROM YOUR PLANET?

NO WAY! THOSE DIAMONDS ARE ALL MINE!

Jupiter is named for the Roman king of the gods because it was said to be the king of the planets.

Jupiter and Saturn are known as the gas giants.

THE SATURN RING ROCKS GO ROUND AND ROUND . . .

Some of the pieces of ice and rock in Saturn's rings are as tiny as grains of sand. Others are as big as houses.

Because of the kinds of gases that make up Saturn, the planet might be able to float in a tub of water—if you could find one big enough!

THIS IS THE BIGGEST BATH TUB WE COULD FIND. LET'S SEE IF IT FITS!

I'M IN THE MOOD FOR A NICE, WARM BATH.

Jupiter has 79 moons that we know of. Saturn has 82— the most in our solar system.

Now That's Cold!

In the cold, dark outer reaches of our solar system, the last two gas planets orbit the sun from really, *really* far away. They are known as the ice giants. First is Uranus, at about 1.8 billion miles (2.9 billion km) from the sun. Uranus is unlike any other planet because it spins on its side. Another 1 billion miles (1.6 billion km) beyond Uranus, stormy Neptune has winds that blow nine times stronger than the fiercest winds on Earth!

Uranus may have tipped on its side when an Earth-sized object crashed into it long ago.

OUCH! THAT'S GONNA LEAVE A MARK!

Uranus has our solar system's most extreme seasons. As it orbits, the side not facing the sun has a 21-year winter!

Uranus has 27 moons that we know of. Some are named after William Shakespeare characters.

Scientists knew Neptune was there before they ever saw it. They noticed a **wobble** in Uranus's orbit caused by Neptune's gravity.

DON'T BE JEALOUS, TRITON. YOU'RE STILL THE BIGGEST!

HEY, NEPTUNE! WHAT DO YOU NEED SO MANY MOONS FOR?

Neptune has 14 known moons. The largest is called Triton.

Both Uranus and Neptune have **rings**, but they're hard to see.

I'VE NEVER SEEN THEIR RINGS.

I HAVE!

HUSH, YOU TWO! WE'LL ALL GET TO SEE THE RINGS ONCE WE GET CLOSER!

Pluto the Dwarf Planet

Way out past Neptune is tiny, cold, dark Pluto. Pluto was discovered in 1930. It was considered the ninth planet until 2006, when scientists decided it was only a dwarf planet. Why? Because, unlike the eight planets in our solar system, Pluto's gravity isn't strong enough to clear away other similar-sized objects in its orbit. Poor little Pluto!

It takes 248 Earth years for Pluto to orbit the sun.

Pluto is only about **half the width of the United States.**

C'MON, PLUTO! YOU CAN DO IT. FINISH THE ORBIT!

UGH, I STILL HAVE 23 YEARS TO GO!

Shortly after Pluto was discovered, an 11-year-old girl picked its name. The planet was named for the Roman god of the underworld.

ARE YOU PROUD OF YOUR DWARF PLANET?

I'D RATHER HAVE A REAL PLANET NAMED AFTER ME!

Pluto has five moons. The largest, Charon, is half the size of Pluto!

Along with Pluto, there are four other known dwarf planets in our solar system: Ceres, Eris, Haumea, and Makemake.

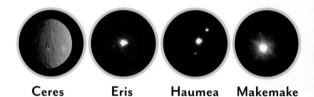

Ceres   Eris   Haumea   Makemake

Some scientists think Pluto should be made a full planet again. The battle over the tiny Pluto rages on!

Many Marvelous Moons

The eight planets of our solar system are each amazing in their own ways, but their many moons are incredible, too! Moons orbit planets, but some are so large that they'd be considered planets themselves if they orbited stars instead. Other moons are just a few miles across. Some moons have their own atmospheres, and some have oceans hidden beneath their surfaces. Let's go moon hopping!

The largest moon in our solar system is Jupiter's Ganymede. It's bigger than Mercury!

Callisto

Europa

Ganymede

Io

I SEE YOU, GANYMEDE!

LET'S HIDE, QUICK! GALILEO IS AFTER US!

Astronomer Galileo Galilei spotted four moons around Jupiter in 1610. Ganymede, Io, Callisto, and Europa are called Galilean **satellites**, after the man who discovered them.

Saturn's moon Titan has a planet-like atmosphere and liquid on its surface. This makes it one of the places most similar to Earth that has been discovered so far!

LOOK HOW FAR I'VE COME!

A spacecraft landed on Titan in 2005. At the time, this was the farthest any spacecraft had traveled from Earth!

Saturn's moon Hyperion **looks like a giant sponge.**

Saturn's moon Enceladus **shoots fountains of ice crystals** from an underground ocean.

YOU LOOK JUST LIKE ME!

WHO ARE YOU CALLING A MONSTER?

Uranus's moon Miranda is called **the Frankenstein moon.** It looks like it's made of different pieces, like Frankenstein's monster!

In Search of Exoplanets

If the planets and moons of our solar system aren't enough for you, there's more to discover! Scientists think there are 100 billion other planets throughout our **galaxy**. And there are at least 100 billion galaxies in the universe, each with their own planets! These planets orbiting stars other than our sun are called exoplanets. Scientists are discovering more every year. Could there be an exoplanet out there just like Earth? Maybe you'll be the one to find out!

Images from a big telescope in space show thousands of galaxies. See the tiny dots? Those are galaxies!

LOOK AT ALL THOSE OTHER GALAXIES WITH EXOPLANETS IN SPACE!

I WONDER IF ANYONE OUT THERE IS LOOKING AT US RIGHT NOW!

Exoplanets come in many forms. Scientists have discovered some with oceans of lava. They've also found one that is light and puffy.

I HAVE A HEART OF GOLD . . . UMM, I MEAN DIAMOND.

Scientists have found an exoplanet where a year lasts less than 18 hours. The planet may have a core made of diamond!

Scientists have discovered more than 4,000 exoplanets.

There's even an exoplanet with its own moon!

LOOK AT THAT DISTANT STAR. IT HAS EIGHT PLANETS. ONE IS CALLED EARTH.

I WONDER IF ANYONE LIVES THERE!

Cratered Moon
Craft Project

Now that you've learned about our solar system's amazing planets and some of their incredible moons, it's time to create your very own moon. You can look up at Earth's moon for inspiration and make your clay moon as cratered as you like!

The moon's craters come from space objects smashing into it.

What You Will Need

- A string
- A firm foam ball
- Air-dry clay
- Rocks
- Black paint
- A sponge

The moon's largest crater is 1,500 miles (2,400 km) wide. That's the distance from New York to Texas!

Step One

Tie the string around the foam ball.

Step Two

Roll the clay into a thick pancake shape. Wrap it around the foam ball, and smooth out all the creases.

Step Three

Take a rock and press it into the clay hard enough to leave a dent. Repeat with other rocks. You can use the pointy ends and wider sides of different rocks to make different craters. Leave the clay to dry.

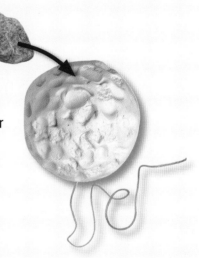

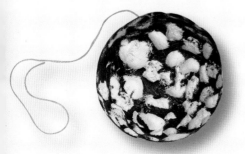

Step Four

Put some paint on the sponge. Rub it on your moon, being careful not to get paint in the craters. Leave it to dry. Hang your moon up to display it!

Glossary

acid a chemical that can be dangerous to humans

asteroids rocks found in space

astronomers scientists who study space

atmosphere the gases surrounding a planet

carbon dioxide a colorless, odorless gas

core the center part of a planet or other space body

disk a thin, flat, round shape

galaxy a collection of billions of stars and other matter held together by gravity

gravity the force that pulls things toward Earth, the sun, or other large objects in space

material physical matter that makes up objects

orbits moves in a path around another object; the path is also called an orbit

oxygen a colorless, odorless gas people need to live

rovers vehicles for exploring the surface of a planet or moon

satellites objects in space that orbit larger objects

sphere a perfectly round, solid shape

wobble to move or tip from side to side

Read More

Finan, Catherine C. *Stars and Galaxies (X-treme Facts: Space).* Minneapolis: Bearport Publishing, 2022.

Rathburn, Betsy. *Planets (Torque: Space Science).* Minneapolis: Bellwether Media, 2019.

Sommer, Nathan. *The Moon (Torque: Space Science).* Minneapolis: Bellwether Media, 2019.

Learn More Online

1. Go to **www.factsurfer.com** or scan the QR code below.

2. Enter **"Planets and Moons"** into the search box.

3. Click on the cover of this book to see a list of websites.

Index

About the Author

Catherine C. Finan is a writer living in northeastern Pennsylvania. One of her most-prized possessions is a telescope that lets her peer into space.